Kenneth Grahame's The Wind in the Willows

Written by Kenneth Grahame

Adapted by Margaret McAllister

Illustrated by Daron Parton

Published by Pearson Education Limited, Edinburgh Gate, Harlow, Essex, CM20 2JE.

www.pearsonschools.co.uk

Text © Margaret McAllister 2013
Original illustrations © Pearson Education Limited 2013
Illustrated by Daron Parton, Pickled Ink
Designed by Vincent Shaw-Morton

The right of Margaret McAllister to be identified as author of this work has been asserted by her in accordance with the Copyright, Designs and Patents Act 1988.

First published 2013

17 16 15 14 13
10 9 8 7 6 5 4 3 2 1

British Library Cataloguing in Publication Data
A catalogue record for this book is available from the British Library

ISBN 978 0 435 14411 1

Copyright notice
All rights reserved. No part of this publication may be reproduced in any form or by any means (including photocopying or storing it in any medium by electronic means and whether or not transiently or incidentally to some other use of this publication) without the written permission of the copyright owner, except in accordance with the provisions of the Copyright, Designs and Patents Act 1988 or under the terms of a licence issued by the Copyright Licensing Agency, Saffron House, 6–10 Kirby Street, London EC1N 8TS (www.cla.co.uk.) Applications for the copyright owner's written permission should be addressed to the publisher.

Printed and bound in Dubai by Oriental Press.

Acknowledgements
We would like to thank Bangor Central Integrated Primary School, Northern Ireland; Bishop Henderson Church of England Primary School, Somerset; Bletchingdon Parochial Church of England Primary School, Oxfordshire; Brookside Community Primary School, Somerset; Bude Park Primary School, Hull; Carisbrooke Church of England Primary School, Isle of Wight; Cheddington Combined School, Buckinghamshire; Dair House Independent School, Buckinghamshire; Deal Parochial School, Kent; Glebe Infant School, Gloucestershire; Henley Green Primary School, Coventry; Lovelace Primary School, Surrey; Our Lady of Peace Junior School, Slough; Tackley Church of England Primary School, Oxfordshire; and Twyford Church of England School, Buckinghamshire for their invaluable help in the development and trialling of the Bug Club resources.

Every effort has been made to contact copyright holders of material reproduced in this book. Any omissions will be rectified in subsequent printings if notice is given to the publishers.

Contents

Chapter 1
The River Bank   5
Chapter 2
The Open Road   14
Chapter 3
Wild Wood   22
Chapter 4
Mr Badger   30
Chapter 5
Home   35
Chapter 6
Mr Toad   46
Chapter 7
Toad's Adventures   56
Chapter 8
Further Adventures of Toad   64
Chapter 9
Mr Badger's Plans   77
Chapter 10
The Return of Mr Toad   86

CHAPTER ONE
The River Bank

Mole had been working hard all morning, spring-cleaning his little home. He had scrubbed until his back ached, and then painted until his arms were tired, but the fresh spring air wriggled into the underground tunnels until he gave up, threw down his paint brush and ran outside.

How wonderful to be in the sunshine at last! he thought. The breeze and the birdsong were everywhere around him. He trotted across the meadow, loving the freedom – this was spring without the cleaning!

Thinking what a treat it was to have a holiday, he ran on further than he had ever run in all his life until he came to a river.

A river! He had never seen one before! It was like a long, swerving animal, winding its way between the banks, sparkling, gurgling and laughing to itself. The astonished Mole sat down and stared at it.

From the other side of the river, something glinted. Mole wasn't quite sure what it was, but when it disappeared and appeared again, he began to think it was an eye and that somebody was watching him. It winked, and the whiskery face of a water rat popped out from a hole in the riverbank.

"Oh!" said Mole. He had seen the water rat round and about but, as Rat lived on the river bank and Mole was an underground fellow, they had never stopped for a conversation.

"Hello, Water Rat!"

"Hello, Mole!" said Rat. "Would you like to come over and join me?"

Mole was about to complain that he couldn't swim when for the first time he noticed a small blue and white boat, just the size for two animals.

Rat rowed it expertly across to Mole, who stepped in cautiously, holding tightly to Rat's paw. For an underground animal who had never been in a boat in his life, it was a great adventure.

The boat swayed gently as Rat began to row, and Mole waggled his toes in contentment.

"There's nothing," said Rat as he pulled on the oars, "absolutely nothing half so much worth doing as simply messing about in boats – or with boats, in or out of them! It doesn't matter where you're going, or even whether you get there. I've packed a picnic and it's far too much for one animal. Let's make a day of it!"

For the first time, Mole saw the picnic hamper under the seats. The size of it awoke his curiosity.

"It's a very big hamper," he observed.

"Do you think so?" asked Rat. "It's only what I always take for these little trips. Isn't the river glorious? To me, it's my family and

my world! And it's always busy, what with kingfishers, otters and of course the moorhens dabbling about."

"What's over there?" asked Mole, pointing to some dark woodland on the opposite side.

"That's Wild Wood," said Rat shortly. "We don't go there."

"What's the matter with it?" asked Mole.

"It's – er – well, some of the animals there – you understand – mostly they behave, but they can be – troublesome. Having said that, Badger lives there and he's the best of animals. And none of them would dare bother him. I don't go there and neither should you."

Mole could tell that Rat didn't wish to discuss Wild Wood any further and said no more about it. They came to a lake where Rat moored the boat and they carried the picnic hamper on to the grass.

"May I unpack it?" asked Mole shyly.

"Of course you can!" said Rat, who sprawled on the grass while the delighted Mole unwrapped the little packages from the basket. "It's not much," he said, "just some coldbeef coldchickenandsalad, sandwichespickledcucumbersfrenchbread, gingerbeerlemonade …"

"Oh, my!" cried Mole. When the feast was spread out, he said 'Oh my!' again in delight. He had started early on his spring cleaning and been out in the fresh air for hours, so when Rat told him 'pitch in!', he was very glad to obey. The two animals were just finishing a very good lunch when Mole asked, "Who's that?"

"Oh, hello, Otter!" said Rat. Otter scrambled up the bank and shook the water from his coat.

"Hello, you two!" said Otter cheerfully. "Look out; Toad's on the river today! He's got a new rowing boat this time."

"Toad's always got some new craze," Rat told Mole. "He used to like sailing boats, but he never sticks with anything for long. He'll soon get bored with rowing boats. Look, there he goes!"

Mole saw a short, stout animal rowing

a small boat with all his might. There was a lot of splashing, and the boat pitched dangerously from side to side.

"He'll turn the boat over if he rows like that," remarked Rat. "He loves going too fast, and it never turns out well. Time for us to pack up."

They packed the hamper and Mole settled down in the boat to watch as Rat rowed. The more he watched, the more he thought how easy it looked.

"May I row, please?" he asked.

Rat smiled kindly, but he shook his head. "It's not as easy as it looks," he said. "You'll need a few lessons first."

Mole said nothing, but restlessness was creeping into him and he longed to row. Jealousy grew inside him until the idea that he could row, and that Rat really should let him have a turn, completely overwhelmed him. He leapt forward and caught the oars so suddenly that Rat fell over backwards.

"Don't!" called Rat, but it was too late.

Mole dug at the water with the oars, missed, fell on top of Rat and grabbed wildly at the side of the boat. With a *sploosh!* they overturned.

Cold river water rushed over Mole and filled his ears as he sank. Then the Water Rat was holding him up, pulling him to the shore and laughing.

"Trot up and down to get warm!" said Rat. "I'll dive for the boat!"

When Rat had dived for the boat, the oars and the picnic hamper, he helped the wet and thoroughly ashamed Mole back into the boat. Mole shivered.

"I'm so sorry, Rat!" he sniffed. "Please forgive me!"

"That's all right!" laughed good-natured Rat. "What's a little wet to a water rat? Come with me and get dry – come and stay, if you like!"

In Rat's snug home in the riverbank, dry clothes were found for Mole, and in the evening they sat in armchairs by a blazing fire while Rat told stories of the riverbank. At last, sleepy Mole went to bed and fell asleep contentedly to the sound of the river lapping on the window.

CHAPTER TWO
The Open Road

As Rat was so welcoming, and Mole so enjoyed his new way of life on the river, Mole stayed for weeks at Rat's riverbank house. By the time he had learned to row and become used to the ways of the river, he felt he had lived there all his life. One fine morning, he asked Rat, "May I meet Mr Toad? I keep hearing about him."

"We'll go to Toad Hall today!" said Rat. "There's always a welcome from Toad. He's not clever, and he's always boasting, but a nice enough animal all the same. And extremely rich."

Toad Hall was an elegant old manor with gardens and a boat house. They arrived to find Toad enjoying the sun in the garden, and he hurried to meet them and shake their paws without waiting to be introduced to Mole.

"How delightful to see you!" he exclaimed in great excitement. "I've got something to tell you! I've discovered the best kind of travel ever! No more boats! No more river! Come and see this!"

He led them to the stable yard. Beside the stables stood a gleaming little gipsy caravan painted bright canary-yellow, with green edging and flourishes, and red wheels.

"Travelling the open road!" announced Toad. "Moving on every day, the heath, the downs, villages, towns, cities! Come and look inside!"

Mole hurried eagerly into the caravan but Rat stood silently outside with his paws firmly in his pockets. The caravan was fitted with tables, bunks, a stove, cupboards and all the pots and pans anyone could need.

"All ready to go!" said Toad, opening doors. "All the food we need, drinks, games – all ready for when we start this afternoon!"

"Excuse me," said Rat slowly. "But did I hear you say 'we' … and 'start' … and 'this afternoon'?"

"Now, Ratty, you know you have to come!" insisted Toad. "I can't manage without you! You don't want to stick to your damp home and your old river, do you?"

"Yes I do," replied Rat. "And so does Mole, don't you, Mole?"

"Oh, yes!" said Mole loyally, but he couldn't help gazing at the caravan.

"Let's talk about it over some lunch," suggested Toad.

Mole was not used to Toad. Over an excellent lunch, Toad enthused about the wonderful adventures they would have travelling the open road until even Rat was reluctantly persuaded to go along. The caravan was all ready but the horse was not and resented being chased round the meadow. Finally it was harnessed and they set out on their journey, taking turns to ride or walk through the pleasant little lanes. At last, they ate supper outside and fell sleepily into the little bunks in the caravan.

"This is the life!" yawned Toad. "Talk about your old river!"

"I don't talk about it," said Rat quietly. "But," he added, so softly that only Mole heard, "I think about it. All the time."

Mole squeezed his paw. "We don't have to stay, Ratty!" he whispered. "Shall we run away, back to the river?"

"No, we'll stay," Rat whispered back. "Toad isn't safe to be left alone. He'll soon get tired of this and we can go home."

It happened a great deal sooner than they had expected.

The next morning Toad slept in, so Rat and Mole lit the fire and cooked breakfast. Toad appeared when the work was all done, saying that life on the road was delightfully simple.

For the rest of that day they made him do his share of the work, and the next morning it took both of them to haul him out of his bunk. By that afternoon, they had left the quiet country lanes and were on their first main road.

Mole was walking beside the horse to keep him company and Toad was talking to Rat, who wasn't listening, when from far behind them came a faint humming like the buzzing of a bee. They turned to see a cloud of dust on the road.

"Poop-poop!" called something faintly, and a storm of dust and a roar of noise sent them leaping for the nearest ditch as a shining motor car rushed past them. The horse bolted with the caravan lurching behind it until it toppled on the edge of the ditch, fell and smashed.

"Road hogs!" shouted Rat, climbing out of the ditch. "Villains! Highwaymen!" The car was well out of sight by now and Mole was calming the terrified horse, but Toad sat quite still in the middle of the road.

"Come on, Toad," said Rat. "Let's get you home now."

But Toad only stared ahead of him. At last, he spoke.

"Poop-poop!" he murmured happily. "Glorious! What a way to travel! How exciting! I will speed round the country in a cloud of dust, scattering silly little caravans! Who wants a caravan? Poop-poop!"

"He's off again," said Rat wearily. "He's got a new idea. It's cars now. Give me a hand, Mole; we have to get him home."

It was a long, tiring plod to the nearest station and the train home. Mole and Rat left Toad at Toad Hall, took their boat from the boat house and rowed back to Rat's riverbank home.

The next afternoon, Rat came home from a day's pottering about on the river.

"Is there any news of Toad?" asked Mole.

"Oh, plenty of it," sighed Rat. "It's what all the animals are talking about. He's been to town and ordered a car. A large and very expensive one."

CHAPTER THREE
Wild Wood

Mole very much wanted to meet Badger, who was highly respected along the river. He often asked Rat if they could invite him to dinner at River Bank, but Rat always said, "It's no good inviting Badger, or calling on him either. He'll turn up some day or other, when he feels like it."

But Badger never did turn up, as summer and autumn ran their course. As winter approached the river was too fast and full for boats and Rat slept a great deal. So one afternoon, as Rat dozed by the fire, Mole slipped out to try an adventure of his own.

He would explore Wild Wood and maybe even meet Badger.

Under the steely winter sky the countryside was stripped down to its bare bones; leafless, fine and strong.

Mole passed into Wild Wood where there was no sound but the cracking of twigs under his paws and ran on into the darkness of the wood. All was still.

Then the faces began.

He thought he glimpsed somebody watching him. Was it there, or wasn't it? Was that a face – an evil, pointed little face in a tree trunk? It was there, then it wasn't. Then there was another! Or was it? Yes! No! Every tree seemed to show him a sharp little face, full of malice, and to escape them he swerved from the path and into the untrodden wood.

Then the whistling began.

It came from somewhere behind him and he hurried forward, further into the deep darkness of the trees. Now the whistling was in front of him, now it was on either side – whoever it was, they were closing in on him.

He was alone, unarmed, and completely lost, as the night closed in on Wild Wood with its watching faces and whistling calls all around him.

Then the pattering began.

It was the scuttling of little feet – *pat-pat-pat*. Were they behind him, or in front? Now they were all around, running, hunting, chasing, and in panic Mole began to run. He stumbled, he bumped into things, he dodged and darted and, finally, exhausted and terrified, he threw himself into the hollow of a tree. There, he curled among the leaves while the terror of Wild Wood whistled and pattered around him.

By the warmth of the fire in his riverbank house, Rat woke up and wondered where Mole had gone. When he saw that Mole's cap and smart new boots were missing, he went to the front door and looked for prints in the muddy ground. There was no doubt about it. The trail led to Wild Wood. Rat frowned, took his coat and a strong stick, and walked out into the night.

When Rat strode into Wild Wood with his determined air and his stick, the faces, whistling and pattering died away. He searched the wood, calling Mole's name until from under a tree came a frightened little voice –

"Ratty? Is that you?"

Rat dived under the tree. Mole was still tired out and still terrified.

"That was a silly thing to do!" said Rat, but he said it kindly. "You shouldn't come here on your own, Mole, especially as you don't know Wild Wood. Have a little rest, and then we'll get home."

By the time they had rested, though, snow was falling steadily. Soon every tree trunk and fallen branch was covered in light snow, and nothing looked the same as it had before. The animals guessed at the right way to go, weren't sure, found that every path and every tree trunk looked the same and finally knew that they were completely lost.

"We'll never get home tonight," admitted Rat at last. "And the snow's getting too deep to go on. There's a dell down there, and the ground is humpy and hummocky, so if we go into that we might find a cave or something – somewhere to stay until morning."

They explored the bumpy ground, looking for somewhere dry and sheltered. They were investigating a snowy mound when Mole tripped over and fell on his face.

"Ow!" he cried, and sat up, clutching his leg. "I hurt my shin!"

"Poor Mole!" said Rat. "Let's have a look at it. You've cut it quite badly, haven't you? Let me see – oh! I wonder what tripped you up, Mole? It must have been something with a sharp edge."

"Who cares?" said Mole crossly. "It hurts."

Rat knelt down in the snow. He scraped, scrabbled about with his paws and then began to dig furiously.

"Oh, come on, Rat!" complained Mole.

"Hooray!" cried Rat, dancing for joy. "Hooray, come and see this!"

Mole got up grumpily to see what Rat had found.

"It's a boot scraper," he said. "So what? Somebody must have left it lying around, just where an animal can trip over it."

"Oh, Mole!" said Rat, and scraped a bit more. "Come and help! Now, look! What's *that*?"

"A door mat," grumbled Mole. "You appear to have dug up a rubbish heap. We can't eat a door mat and we can't sleep in it, either. Perhaps when you've finished dancing round it, we can find somewhere to sleep."

"A door mat!" said Rat. "Doesn't it tell you anything?"

"Of course it doesn't – it's a doormat," grumbled Mole. "They're not supposed to tell you things."

"Oh, Mole!" cried Rat, who was getting angry. "Just dig!"

He dug so hard that Mole gave up sulking and joined in, and together they scraped away the snow until something else appeared. They had found a dark green door, with a doorbell and a brass plate –

MR BADGER

"Ratty!" exclaimed Mole. "You are a genius! You worked it all out! You saw a door scraper and you thought, 'there must be a doormat'! And then, you clever animal, you thought ..."

"Oh, just ring the bell," said Rat. So Mole rang the bell, Rat hammered with his stick and, at last, they heard the clunk of the bolt being drawn back.

CHAPTER FOUR
Mr Badger

The door opened a few inches. A long snout appeared and a pair of sleepy eyes.

"Now, what is this about?" asked a gruff, stern voice.

"It's only us! Please let us in!" pleaded Rat. "It's Rat and Mole, and we're lost!"

"Ratty!" said Badger kindly. "In the snow! In Wild Wood! Come in, both of you!"

Badger wore an old dressing gown and shabby slippers and looked ready for bed, but he didn't seem to mind their arrival at all. He led them through winding underground tunnels to a warm kitchen with long seats before the bright fire, where he helped them to pull off their wet boots and coats. In the warmth and safety of the firelit kitchen, it soon seemed that the terror of Wild Wood was long ago and far away, and the supper Badger put before them was so welcome and so generous that soon Rat and Mole felt completely at home, warm and full.

"Now, what's the news?" asked Badger. "How's Toad?"

"Terrible," said Rat. "He'd be all right if he paid a sensible animal to drive him, but he insists on driving himself and he's hopeless. He's smashed up six cars and he's on to the seventh."

"He's been in hospital three times," said Mole.

"And what with the cars he buys, and the fines for dangerous driving, he's running through his money," said Rat. "We need to do something."

"We must," agreed Badger. "But not in winter!"

Rat and Mole understood. Winter was a time for keeping warm and sleeping, not for action.

"We'll take him in hand when the year has turned," said Badger. "Rat, you're half asleep already. Come along, the two of you, and I'll show you where you can sleep. Get up as late as you like!"

When Mole and Rat came to breakfast the next morning, two small hedgehogs were sitting at the table enjoying hot porridge. They had got lost in the snow on the way to school, they explained, and knew that Badger's house was a safe place to go. Badger had gone to his study to attend to important business, which probably meant a morning sleep, as badgers do not like to be busy in winter. He appeared in time for lunch and talked very kindly to Mole over the meal. They were both underground animals, and so had plenty to talk about.

"I do like being well down under the earth," said Mole. "It feels safe to me."

"Exactly!" said Badger, beaming. "If you need more space, you dig another tunnel. The weather's no bother underground. Rat has to move house every time the river floods."

"I know," said Rat, "but I need to be back there. I always think the river might run away if I'm not there to look after it. We should get out of Wild Wood in daylight."

"You can go through my tunnels," said Badger. "There's a short cut all the way to the edge of the wood. And don't worry about the Wild Wooders. They know better than to bother me."

Badger was quite right. They found their way home without getting lost, and without as much as a glimpse of a Wild Wooder. Soon they were back at Rat's home, with the fire dancing in the hearth and the sound of the river rippling past the window.

CHAPTER FIVE
Home

On a frosty afternoon in December, when sheep huddled together for warmth, Mole and Rat were hurrying along beside a field. They had enjoyed a day exploring the uplands and were far from home and eager to get back to River Bank before dark.

"We're coming to a village," warned Mole. The animals were shy of places where people lived closely together.

"Never mind!" said Rat. "They won't notice us. They'll all be sitting round their fireplaces, keeping warm. We can take a peek through their windows and see what they're doing."

Light, powdery snow lay on the ground, and from every cottage glowed the warmth of firelight. The two animals looked through the windows to see families gathered round the table, eating, talking and laughing. In one little window the blind was drawn, but the light behind it showed the clear silhouette of a bird in a cage as it stretched, yawned and shook its feathers. Then wind and sleet flew harshly against the weary animals, and they realised again that they were outside in the winter afternoon and a long way from their own fireside. They turned and scurried away with tired legs and frozen paws.

Rat led the way as darkness fell, his eyes on the grey track. Mole was following, thinking of supper and a good fire, when the call reached him on the air.

It was a faint scent on the wind, but to Mole it was more like the cry of a voice. It reached him in the darkness, and before he knew what it was he had to stop, twitching his nose. He caught it again, and the memory flooded over him.

Home! He must be near his old home! It was near; it was calling to him as if it reached out with little invisible hands, tugging at him to come back to it. It was small and shabby, but it was his own home, and now that he had smelt it again, his whole heart yearned for it. He felt that it had missed him and was begging him to return.

"Ratty!" he called in excitement. "Hold on, Ratty! Come back!"

"Come along, Mole!" called Rat cheerfully, not looking back.

"Please, Ratty!" called Mole. "Please stop! We're so near to my old home, I can smell it, and it's calling me! I must go to it! My *home*! Please, Ratty, oh please, please, stop!"

Rat was too far ahead to hear all that Mole said, or to catch the pleading in his voice. He could smell snow on the air.

"Can't stop now, Mole, whatever it is!" he called back. "Whatever you've found, we'll come and look for it tomorrow! I need your nose to sniff out the path!"

Poor Mole stood in the road and a sob, too

big to hold, gathered up inside him – but he would not abandon Rat. With a wrench that tore at his heart, he turned his back on the scent of his home and pattered on after Rat.

"That's better!" said Rat. "When we're home we'll get a good fire blazing and have supper."

Mole could not speak. It was all he could do to put one paw after another.

At last, Rat noticed his silence and weariness.

"Sit down, Mole," he said. "You're too tired even to talk. Poor old you. Take a rest; it's not far now."

Mole sat down on a tree stump and tried to be brave, but that great sob of distress was still there. It rose up and escaped, and another sob followed, and another, as the poor Mole gave way to his grief. It was all over now. His home was too far away, and his tears could not be stopped. He sat crying helplessly.

The astonished Rat waited for him to become a little quieter. Then he said kindly,

"What is it, old fellow? What can I do to help?"

Still sobbing, Mole tried to speak.

"It's only small and plain," he said, still gulping down tears, " – not like your lovely house – or Badger's – but it was my little home, and I loved it – and I smelt it. It was calling to me on the road – it was near – oh, I wanted it so much! And it wanted me! I tried to tell you – if we could have just gone for a look – but you wouldn't stop!" He collapsed into sobs again.

Rat patted him on the shoulder. "What a mean, selfish fellow I've been!" he muttered. He waited until Mole was calmer, and then set off again, back the way they had come.

"Off we go then!" he called. "Let's find your home!"

"No!" cried Mole. "You were looking forward to River Bank and your supper!"

"Hang supper!" said Rat cheerfully. "Lead the way, Mole!"

With his nose twitching, and with plenty of encouragement from Rat, Mole led the way back. He stopped, sniffed, ran a little way uncertainly and sniffed again. This time, he was sure of the scent. With Rat following, he ran across a field and along a hedge, and then dived into a tunnel. Rat found it long and stuffy, but they came out at last in a wide, sandy courtyard. Mole lifted a lantern from the wall and lit it.

The yard was cold and neglected, but there were garden seats, baskets of trailing ferns, statues and even a little pond edged with cockle shells, where goldfish swam. Beyond it was a small front door with 'Mole End' written on it, and Mole beamed with joy as he opened it and led the way indoors.

He lit a lamp in the hall and looked round at his old home, but the sight of it, dusty and neglected, led him to despair again. Poor Mole sat down with his nose in his paws and looked ready to break into fresh tears.

"Oh, Ratty!" he cried. "I've brought you to this cold, empty place! It's so small and shabby, and you could have been comfortable at River Bank!"

Rat paid no attention to him. He ran about, lighting lamps.

"What a delightful little house!" he said. "I'll get a fire going – is this the sitting-room? I do like the bunks in the wall. What a good idea! Give the table a quick dusting, Mole!"

"But there's nothing for your supper!" wailed Mole. "You poor cold, hungry animal!"

"Oh, we'll find something!" insisted Rat. "Let's forage about!"

Rat soon had a cheerful fire blazing in the hearth, and Mole began to feel better. In a hunt through the cupboards they found a tin of sardines, biscuits and some bottles of ginger beer, and they were ready to eat when there was a scuffling noise outside and a little voice said, "Ready? One, two, three!"

"What's that?" asked Rat.

"It's the field mice!" cried Mole. "They always come round carol-singing at this time of year! I used to give them hot drinks and a bit of supper! It's like old times!"

"Let's see, then!" said Rat, and ran to open the door.

A little group of young field mice stood muffled in scarves and coats in the arc of light from a lantern. Pushing their paws into their pockets for warmth and jiggling their feet, they sang the carol they always sang at Christmas –

Here we stand in the cold and the sleet,
Blowing fingers and stamping feet,
Come from far away you to greet –
You by the fire and we in the street –
Bidding you joy in the morning!

"Well sung, youngsters!" exclaimed Rat. "In you come now and get warm!"

"Yes, come to the fire," said Mole. "Come and – oh, Rat! We've got nothing to give them!"

"Leave that to me!" said Rat. Quietly, he had a word with the oldest field mouse, put money into his paw and gave him a basket.

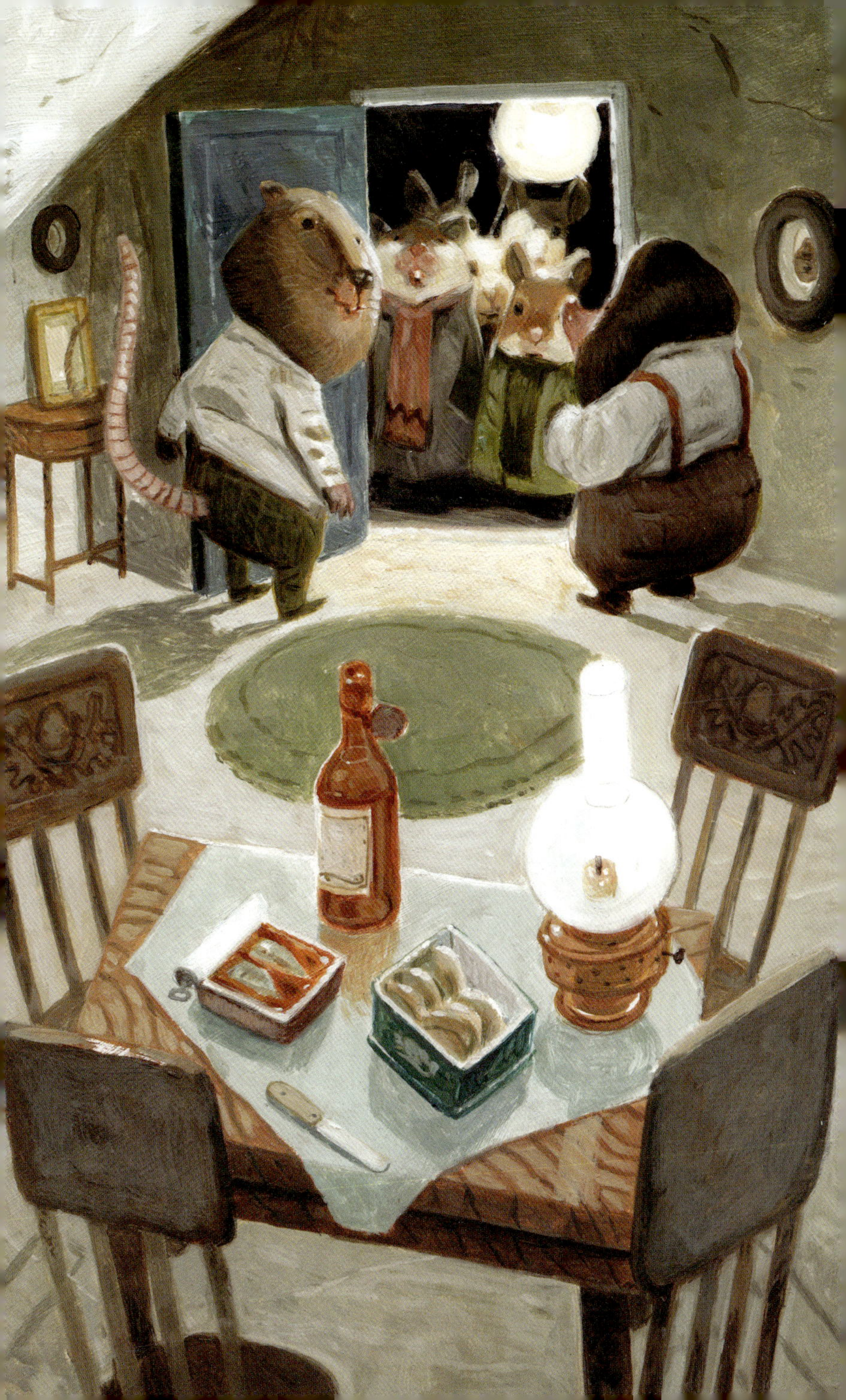

The field mouse trotted away, and the rest of them squashed up together on a bench by the fire, warming their toes and losing their shyness as Mole encouraged them to tell him all about their families. Rat had just made hot drinks for everyone when the field mouse with the basket came back, almost staggering under the weight of the shopping.

Suddenly, the table that had been so bare was set with a glorious supper, and the little field mice forgot that they had ever been cold in their lives. Everyone ate and drank and talked, Mole asked questions about what had been happening while he had been away, and Rat quietly made sure that everyone had plenty to eat and drink and that Mole was happy in his home at last.

At last the field mice went home, all with little treats for their brothers and sisters who were too young for carol-singing, and Rat and Mole finally went to their bunks. Rat wrapped himself in blankets and was asleep in no time, but Mole lay happily awake.

He looked at the room in the firelight and thought how much he loved his home. He knew he would soon go back to River Bank, and he would be happy to do so – but this little place would always wait for him.

CHAPTER SIX
Mr Toad

When winter was over and spring was turning to summer, Rat and Mole were busy on the riverbank getting the boat ready for fine weather. They had been working since dawn and were finishing breakfast when somebody knocked heavily on the door. Mole ran to answer it.

"Mr Badger!" he exclaimed in surprise. Normally, Badger never visited anyone. Rat sat open-mouthed in surprise as Badger strode into the room.

"The hour has come!" announced Badger.

"What hour?" asked Rat.

"Toad's hour!" said Badger. "It's time to take him in hand. I hear he's done nothing but buy cars, crash them and argue with the police all winter. It's time to go along to Toad Hall and teach him some sense."

"Right you are!" said Rat. The animals marched purposefully to Toad Hall, where a shiny new car stood on the drive. As they arrived the front door was thrown open and Toad appeared, wearing the cap, goggles, gauntlets and huge overcoat that he wore for driving.

"Hello, you fellows!" he called heartily. "Let's go ..." But he never finished – Toad, kicking and struggling, was hauled into the house by Rat and Mole.

"Take those ridiculous clothes off him!" ordered Badger.

It proved to be a very difficult task, and Rat had to sit on Toad, but they managed at last to remove Toad's motoring costume and stand him up again.

"Now, Toad," said Badger severely. "You're a good chap at heart and we won't let you go on making a fool of yourself. You're wasting all the money your father left you and giving animals a bad name. Come with me!"

Badger took Toad firmly by the arm, led him into the next room and shut the door. Mole and Rat could hear Badger speaking very sternly and Toad sobbing.

"That's no good!" said Rat. "Talking won't change him!"

When Badger and Toad came out at last, Badger was solemnly leading a tearful Toad by the paw.

Toad looked thoroughly sad and sorry.

"Toad has considered how badly he has been behaving," said Badger. "He is very sorry and promises never to go near a car again. Don't you, Toad?"

There was a long pause. Rat saw a twinkle in Toad's eye.

"No!" said Toad. "I'm not sorry! I was just now, but I'm not any more! The first car I see, I'll drive it away!"

"Then we must use force," said Badger.

"Rat, Mole, lock him in his bedroom!"

"It's for your own good, Toad," said Rat kindly, as they dragged him up the stairs. "Just until you get over this nonsense. No more cars. No more rows with the police."

"No more ending up in hospital," said Mole, as he turned the key.

The animals felt that Toad should never be left alone, so they took turns to stay with him.

At first he would arrange all the chairs into a car and crouch forward, pretending to drive faster and faster until he leapt into the air, turned a somersault and landed on the floor. In time, he stopped this and lay quietly in bed most of the day, but Badger suspected he was planning something.

On a morning when Badger and Mole had gone out, Rat was keeping Toad company. Toad hardly spoke, and when he did his voice was very weak.

"I won't be like this for much longer, Rat," he whispered.

"Good!" said Rat. "Then we can all go to the river again. We don't want to waste such fine boating weather."

"I am afraid I am a great trouble to you," said Toad feebly.

"I'd go to any trouble at all for you," said Rat, "if only you'd be sensible."

"Would you really? But I don't like to be a nuisance," murmured Toad. "I could ask you to run and fetch the doctor – but no. Let nature take its course."

"Why, whatever do you mean?" asked Rat in alarm.

"It may already be too late," sighed Toad.

Rat, growing anxious, looked more carefully at him. Toad didn't seem at all like his old self. He wasn't supposed to leave Toad alone, even for a moment, but it wouldn't take long to fetch the doctor. He hurried outside, locking the door behind him, and ran to the village. As soon as he had gone, Toad laughed, leapt out of bed, got dressed, tied his sheets together and climbed out through the window. He felt extremely proud of himself.

Rat felt very foolish when he came home to find Toad's room empty. He felt even more foolish when he had to explain to Mole and Badger what had happened.

"Goodness knows what he'll do now," grumbled Badger. "At least we don't have to waste time guarding him any longer. Sooner or later, he'll turn up here again, probably between two policemen."

Toad swaggered happily along, telling himself what a clever animal he was. He strode into a little town, found a hotel called *The Red Lion* and ordered lunch. He was halfway through the meal when he heard a sound that made him shiver with excitement.

Poop-poop!

Outside, somebody was parking a car. Presently, the owners came in, laughing and chatting, and settling themselves down for lunch. Toad listened to them talking about the car, until he could no longer bear it.

"I could just go outside and look at it," he thought. He paid his bill and went outside to admire the gleaming car. Nobody else was about.

"I wonder," he said to himself, "if this car starts easily?"

There was only one way to find out. Somehow, as if in a dream, he found himself in the driver's seat.

"I am Toad!" he cried, as he drove out of the yard. "Toad, terror of all traffic!" he shouted, as he sped out of the town.

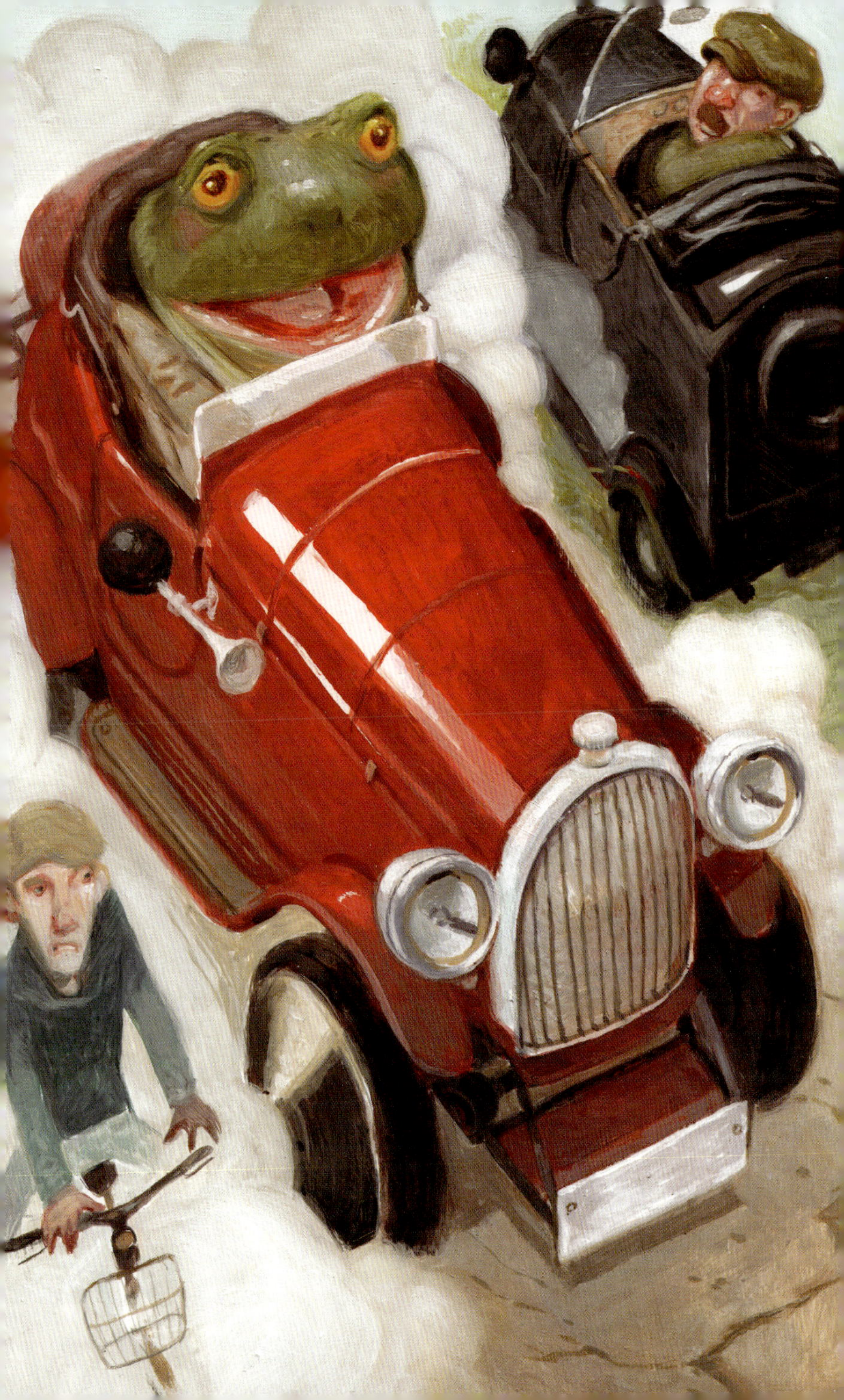

"I am Toad!" he laughed wildly. "Toad of the Road!"

Toad stood in a court room between two police officers. The judge frowned at him.

"Toad," declared the judge, "you have been found guilty of stealing a valuable car, dangerous driving and being extremely cheeky to the police. I wish to make an example of you and give you the harshest sentence I possibly can. You will go to prison for one year for stealing the car and a further three for dangerous driving. However, your most serious offence was the cheek, and you will serve twelve years for that. That comes to – er – nineteen years, I think. May as well make it twenty. Toad, you will spend twenty years in prison."

Toad cried out and begged for mercy, but there was no help for him. Guards loaded him with chains and hauled him away, over a drawbridge and into an ancient castle, past cells and grinning soldiers, further and further from the daylight and into the very heart of the keep. At the door of the grimmest of the grim old dungeons, the jailer pushed him inside and locked him in. Toad was a helpless prisoner in the strongest castle in the whole country.

CHAPTER SEVEN
Toad's Adventures

In the dark, dreary prison, Toad threw himself on the ground and sobbed with self-pity.

How could anyone be so cruel to kind, handsome Toad? he thought. *I will never see my friends again! Poor wretched Toad!*

He mourned and cried for so long that the jailer's daughter felt sorry for him. She brought him tea and toast and the delicious smell of it made Toad feel a little better, then a lot better, and soon he was telling her all about Toad Hall and how magnificent it was and how he was the most important animal on the whole river and all his friends admired him.

Day after day the kind-hearted girl came to visit Toad, and she began to think it was a shame to keep an animal locked in prison. She thought hard about the unfortunate Toad and how she could help him.

"I've an idea," she said one day. "I have an aunt who is a washerwoman."

"Poor you!" said Toad. "Never mind. I'm sure I have aunts who ought to be washerwomen."

"Be quiet – I'm thinking," said the girl. "You talk too much. She comes in tomorrow with the clean washing. I know you have plenty of money. If you pay her, you could swap clothes with her and escape, disguised as a washerwoman. She can pretend you attacked her. You're sure to get away with it. She's short and round, like you."

"Nonsense!" said Toad. "I am very elegant, for a toad."

"Please yourself," said the girl. "Stay in prison if you like."

This made Toad very sorry, and he apologised at once.

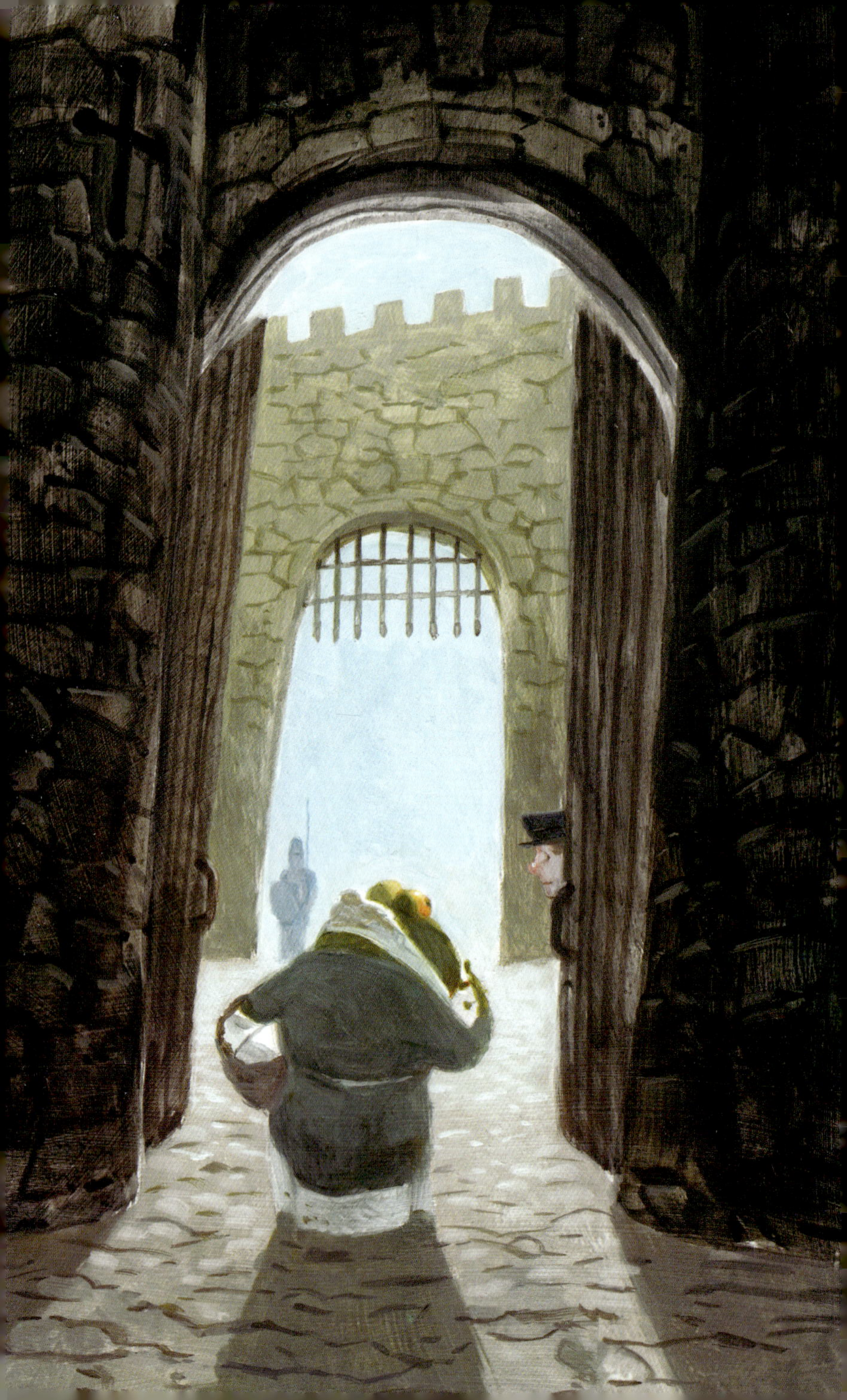

The next time the washerwoman came in, she and Toad exchanged clothes. The girl, giggling, dressed Toad in the dress, shawl and bonnet.

"You look just like Auntie!" she said. "Now off you go and get home safely."

Toad feared very much that the plan would fail and he would be recognised and dragged back to his cell, but he was pleasantly surprised. Everybody seemed to know the washerwoman, and guards stood back to let Toad pass. True, he felt most undignified as he waddled past the warders in a dress and bonnet, and he had to put up with some unwelcome teasing, but door after door opened for him until he found himself outside the prison, wondering where he should go next.

The sound of trains stopping and starting told him that there must be a station nearby and, by following the noise, he found it.

"Lucky me!" he thought. "A station! All I need now is a ticket – and there's the ticket office!"

He was in the ticket queue when he discovered his mistake. His money and keys were in his trousers, and his trousers were back at the prison. He hadn't a penny. He wandered to the platform and gazed at the waiting train with tears of despair and anger trickling down his face. The engine driver noticed him.

"Hello, washerwoman!" he called. "What's the matter?"

"Oh!" said Toad, hoping that he sounded like a washerwoman, "I've lost all my money and I can't buy a ticket to get home to my children! Poor little things! They'll be hungry! Oh, and they might play with matches and set the house on fire!"

"Poor old love," said the engine driver. "Tell you what – if I let you on the train, will you take some washing to do for me?"

"Oh, I'd be delighted!" said Toad. He had never washed a thing in his life, but he could deal with that later.

"Then up you come beside me in the cab," said the driver.

Toad climbed up and sat beside the driver, and soon the train was underway. He was so delighted with his success that he began to sing songs about what a clever Toad he was. The engine driver found this very strange, in a washerwoman.

It wasn't the only strange thing. Soon another train was following them at great speed, and this one was full of policemen waving truncheons and blowing whistles. There were prison guards, too, and men waving walking sticks, and all shouting the same thing.

"Stop!" they yelled. "Stop!"

There was nothing else to do. Toad fell to his knees.

"I confess!" he cried. "I am not a washerwoman! I am Toad, the famous Toad! They threw me into a terrible dungeon and it took all my brilliance and bravery to escape! Now they want to lock me up again – for ever! Save me!"

The driver looked down at him sternly. "What were you in prison for?" he asked.

"I only borrowed a car," wept Toad. "I didn't mean to steal it."

The driver considered. He didn't like cars, but he certainly didn't like policemen chasing his beautiful engine, either.

"You did a bad thing," he said, "but you're an animal in distress, and I won't hand you over. We can't outrun them for ever, but we'll give them a good chase, and where there's a soft place for you to jump off, you jump. I'll tell you when. Ready?"

They piled coal on the fire so that the train rushed forward, rocking on the lines. They shot through a tunnel, plunged into woodland and the driver shouted, "Jump!"

Toad jumped. He landed on soft grass, saw the engine full of policemen rushing past and laughed. But he stopped laughing when he realised that it was late, and getting dark, and he had no idea how to get home. The wood felt strange and frightening. Night birds called, an owl scared him, and there was nothing to eat.

At last he found a hollow tree, made himself as comfortable as he could, slept deeply and woke early in the morning.

He felt better for the sleep, and for a bright morning. He was cold but confident, hungry but hopeful ... but how was he to get home?

CHAPTER EIGHT
Further Adventures of Mr Toad

It was a beautiful fresh morning, and Toad, still in his bonnet, dress and shawl, made his way through the dewy woodland until he came to a road. Nobody was about, Toad had no idea where he was and which way to go, and all he could do was to follow that road and see where it led him. Presently, it came to a canal. A canal, he decided, must be going *from* somewhere *to* somewhere, so he might as well follow it.

Round a bend in the canal came a horse, plodding steadily. It wore a large collar attached to the tow rope of a barge, which glided into view. The only figure on the barge was a large and very strong-looking woman, who was steering.

"Good morning, ma'am!" she called out to Toad.

"I dare say it is," said Toad, pottering along to keep pace with the barge. "But I don't know what to do! I've had a message from my married daughter; she needs me to come to her, and I don't know why! Something must be terribly wrong. Oh, I'm so worried! I know you'll understand, ma'am, if you're a mother yourself. I've had to leave my other children on their own, and now I've lost my way and lost my money, and I don't know what I'll do!"

"Where does your daughter live?" asked the barge-woman.

"Near a house called Toad Hall," replied Toad. "It's very grand."

"I'm going near there," said the kind barge-woman. "I'll give you a lift as far as where the canal meets the road. It's a short walk from there."

Toad stepped on to the barge, thanking her very much, and sat down. He was extremely pleased with himself.

"So you're in the washing business," said the barge-woman, as they travelled. "Are you doing well?"

"Oh, very well!" said Toad. "All the best families send their laundry to me. They know that I thoroughly understand the work. Washing, ironing, starching – I attend to it all personally."

"You do all of that, by yourself?" asked the barge-woman.

"Oh, I have girls who work for me," said Toad airily. "About twenty. But I take a pride in doing things myself."

"You must be very fond of washing," she remarked.

"I love it!" exclaimed Toad. "I'm never so happy as when I have both arms in the washtub. It's a pleasure to me!"

"Now, isn't that lucky?" said the barge-woman to Toad.

"I beg your pardon?" asked Toad nervously.

"I love washing, too," said the barge-woman, "but what with steering and minding the horse, I never have time to do it, and there's such a pile of dirty laundry waiting for me. As you enjoy it so much, you can do a bit as you go along. There's a tub over there and soap, and you can heat water in the kettle."

"Wouldn't you rather wash and I'll steer?" suggested Toad.

The barge-woman laughed. "Steering is harder than it looks," she said. "I'll steer, you can wash, and we'll both be happy."

Toad considered taking a flying leap to the shore, but it was too far. He found the tub, kettle and soap. "Any fool can wash," he told himself.

After half an hour at the washtub, Toad was muttering crossly. He had tried coaxing, slapping and punching the clothes in the soap suds, but none of it did any good. The clothes seemed happy to stay dirty and lay smiling up at him from the water. His back ached, he had lost the soap again, and his smooth

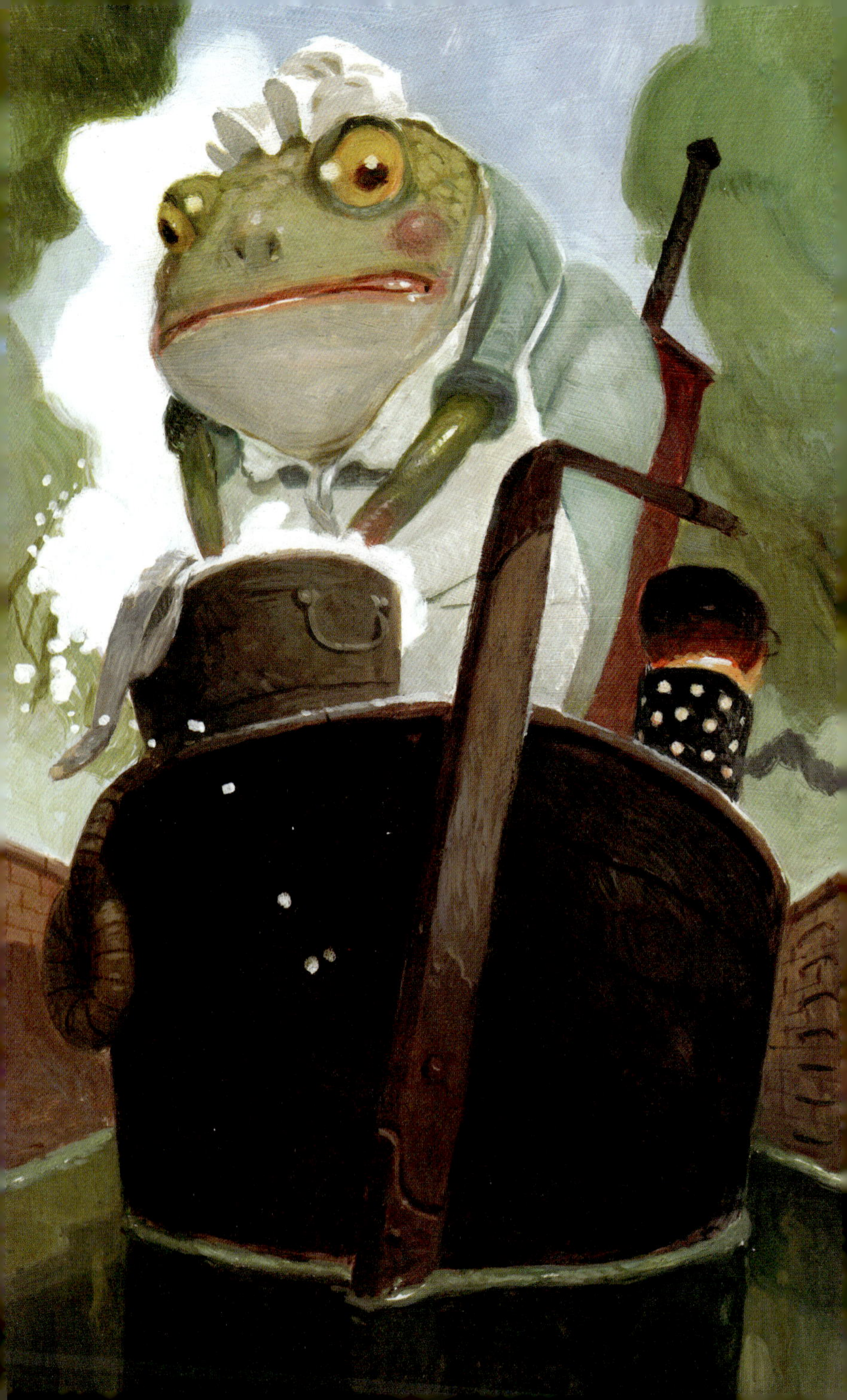

paws had become distressingly crinkly. What was worse was that, suddenly, he could hear laughter! The barge-woman was laughing until she cried.

"I thought so!" she said. "You've never done washing in your life, have you?"

Toad's anger boiled over. "How dare you talk to me like that!" he raged. "You're only a barge-woman! I am Toad – Toad of Toad Hall, no less!"

The woman bent to look under his bonnet.

"So you are!" she cried. "A toad! A horrid, crawly toad on my nice clean barge!"

She let go of the tiller and caught Toad in both hands. Then the world seemed to turn over and over as Toad flew, spinning through the air, and splashed into the canal.

The barge-woman was still laughing as he crawled from the water, dragging his wet skirts behind him and vowing to get even with her.

He pulled his dress over his arm and ran after the barge until he overtook the horse and unhooked the tow rope.

With a jump he was on the horse's back. He urged it to a gallop, steered for the trees and disappeared from view with the bargewoman screaming to him to stop.

The horse was not used to galloping and soon decided to walk instead, but they were well away from the canal. Toad let the horse amble on while he thought of how clever he had been. But a hollow feeling in his stomach reminded him that he had not eaten all day, and he grew desperately hungry.

Toad and the horse travelled aimlessly until they came to a wide stretch of common. A caravan stood there, and, near it, a man sat by a campfire. Hanging over the fire was a cooking pot, and from it came such a rich, warm, savoury smell that Toad felt wild and faint with hunger. He stopped the horse and stared at that pot.

"Want to sell him?" asked the man, with a nod toward the horse.

Toad had not expected this. Perhaps a little horse-trading could help him to the things he desperately wanted – money and a hot breakfast.

"I don't know if I could do that," he said. "He's pure blood – at least, some of him is – but, just if I did decide to sell him, what would you pay?"

"Shilling a leg," said the man.

Toad climbed down from the horse and worked this out on his fingers.

"That's four shillings!" he exclaimed. "Never! I won't take less than six shillings and sixpence, and all I can eat for breakfast!"

The man grumbled, but he shook hands and brought out a bowl and a spoon from the caravan. With a generous hand he poured out a helping of stew so rich and thick that Toad nearly cried at the sight of it.

He ate and ate until he could not manage another mouthful and felt that he had never had such a good breakfast in all his life.

When he had finished and thanked the man, he went on his way. He was himself again, fed, with money in his pocket and bursting with pride. He walked along singing possibly the most conceited song ever composed –

> *The world has held great heroes,*
> *As history books have showed;*
> *But never a name to go down to fame*
> *Compared with that of Toad!*
>
> *The clever men at Oxford*
> *Know all that there is to be knowed,*
> *But they none of them know one half as much*
> *As intelligent Mr Toad!*

There was far more, but it was even worse.

After several miles he reached the main road, where he saw a small dot far away, approaching steadily. A familiar sound fell on his ear. *Poop-poop!*

"This is what I've been missing!" said Toad. "A car! I'll get them to give me a lift and arrive at Toad Hall by car! That'll show Badger!"

He stood at the side of the road ready to wave down the car, but as it drew near his knees turned weak and he collapsed with fear. It was the very car he had stolen from the *The Red Lion*, with the same people in it! They would recognise him and take him back to prison! He lay trembling on the verge, a crumpled heap of misery.

To his horror, the car stopped. A man got out and bent over him.

"It's a poor old washerwoman!" exclaimed the man. "She's not well. We'll take her to the village. There must be somebody there who can look after her."

Toad, delighted with his luck, was loaded into the back seat. Knowing that nobody had recognised him made him bold.

"How are you feeling now, ma'am?" asked somebody.

"Much better, thank you," said Toad feebly. "Perhaps if I could sit in the front beside the driver, the fresh air in my face would do me good."

"How sensible!" said the driver, so Toad was helped into the front seat. All this time, the craving to drive grew upon him.

"Please," he said timidly. "I should like very much to try driving a car. I've been watching most carefully. I would so love to be able to tell my friends that I've done it!"

"What a spirited woman!" said one of the passengers. "Let her try!"

Toad and the driver exchanged seats. Toad listened meekly to all the instructions and gently set the car in motion, remembering that he was supposed to be a washerwoman who had never driven before. As the passengers praised his driving, he speeded up.

"Careful!" said the driver, but it was too late. The car was roaring forward.

"I am Toad!" cried Toad. "Toad, the car

snatcher, the prison breaker!"

"Toad!" repeated the passengers. "Back to prison with him! Grab him!"

It was a pity that they forgot to stop the car first. Toad swerved, to send it crashing through a hedge and into a pond. The impact launched him soaring into the air until, after what seemed like a surprisingly long time, he came to rest in a meadow.

Picking himself up, he ran – but as soon as he thought he was safe he congratulated himself.

"Oh, Toad, you clever fellow!" he said. "Oh, Toad, oh – no!"

Two policemen were running after him. Toad ran, but their legs were long and his were short, and soon they were close. They were almost upon him!

Panicking, glancing over his shoulder, he forgot to look where he was going and *splash!* – he was in the river.

The current was strong and carried him far away. He sank down and came up again, spluttering.

As the river swept him along he saw a hole in the bank, so with both front paws he grabbed at the edge of it and held on, puffing and gasping. He stared down into the hole. Something inside was moving.

"Rat!" panted Toad. "It's you!"

CHAPTER NINE
Mr Badger's Plans

Rat grabbed Toad by the scruff of the neck and hauled him indoors. Once safely inside River Bank, though water streamed from his clothes, Toad started at once to talk about himself.

"I've had such adventures, Ratty!" he began. "I've escaped prison, stolen a horse and sold it, got the better of ..."

"Toad," said Rat firmly, "go upstairs, take off that ridiculous dress and clean yourself up. Wear some of my clothes. And stop showing off."

Toad was about to argue when he caught

sight of himself in a mirror and thought better of it.

When he came down, clean, dry and dressed, he told Rat his adventures, all the time emphasising his own cleverness.

"So, Toad," said Rat when Toad had finished, "why exactly are you so full of yourself? You've been arrested, put in prison, pursued and thrown in the canal. And why? Because you *stole* a car. Crashing cars is bad enough, but stealing!"

"I suppose you're right, Ratty," said Toad humbly, though he was secretly thinking what fun it had all been. "I should calm down now. I'll stroll quietly back home to Toad Hall."

"Toad Hall!" repeated Rat. "You mean you haven't heard?"

"Heard what, Rat?" he asked. "What happened?"

"The stoats and weasels happened," said Rat. "The Wild Wooders. They've taken over Toad Hall."

Toad leaned his head in his hands. Two large tears splashed on to the table.

"Tell me," he said.

"When you were away, a lot of animals said you'd never come back," Rat told him. "But Badger and Mole believed you would, and they moved into Toad Hall to keep it aired and clean, ready for you. Then one awful dark wet night the house was attacked on all sides by stoats, weasels and ferrets from Wild Wood, who took the place by storm. Badger and Mole did their best to fight them off, but they were two against hundreds! They were thrown out and the Wild Wooders have lived there ever since, eating your food, drinking your drink, making jokes about you and wrecking the place."

"Oh, have they?" said Toad, standing up. "I'll see about that!"

"It's no good!" said Rat. "There are hundreds of them, all armed. Don't try to do anything until we've seen Badger and Mole."

"Oh, yes," said Toad. "What happened to them?"

"It's about time you asked," said Rat. "While you were galloping about the country, they have been camping out in all weathers, watching your house and trying to come up with a plan to get Toad Hall back! You don't deserve such friends!"

Toad was about to say that he would go out at once and camp with them when Rat put supper on the table and Toad thought again. They had finished eating when Badger and Mole arrived. Badger solemnly shook Toad's paw, but Mole could not conceal his delight.

"Toad!" he cried. "You're back already! How on earth did you do it?"

Rat tried to intervene, but it was too late. Toad was making the most of his opportunity.

"Oh, I only broke out of the strongest prison in England," he said. "Only captured a railway train and a horse!" He took the money from his pocket. "Only made an excellent deal ..."

"Toad, stop it!" ordered Rat. "Mole, you mustn't encourage him. Have they still got all those guards around Toad Hall?"

Rat, Toad and Mole began talking animatedly about plans for taking Toad Hall when the gruff voice of Badger commanded them all to silence. He rose to his feet.

"Toad," he said, so severely that Toad burst into tears and curled up on the sofa, "think of what your father would say if he could see you now. He was my great friend and the best of animals. And – this is something I have never told you – he told me a secret."

Toad, being fond of secrets, stopped crying and sat up.

"There is an underground passage," continued Badger. "It starts in the riverbank, near here, and emerges in the pantry of Toad Hall."

"Nonsense!" cried Toad. "I know every inch of Toad Hall, and I can promise you there's no secret tunnel."

Badger glared down at him. "Your father was a *wise* animal," he said. "He told me a great deal that he never told you because he knew that you couldn't hold your tongue. He discovered the old hidden passage and had it repaired, in case it should ever be needed. I promised him that I wouldn't tell you about it unless you were in the greatest need. Now, Mole and I have done some spying and the Wild Wooders are having a party tomorrow for the Chief Weasel's birthday. All the Wild Wooders will be in the dining room, eating and drinking, unarmed and suspecting nothing. We make our way through the passage, creep out in the pantry, and ..."

"Rush in on them!" shouted Rat.

"And whack 'em and whack 'em and whack 'em!" cried Toad.

"Exactly!" said Badger. "Now, off to bed with you all."

Toad slept late in the morning and woke to find that Mole had gone out and Rat was busily hurrying about arranging heaps of swords, sticks, cutlasses, bandages and boxes of sticking plasters, while Badger sat in an armchair and read the newspaper. Toad found a strong stick and waved it about.

"I'll learn 'em to steal my house!" he shouted. "I'll learn 'em!"

"Don't say 'learn 'em'," said Ratty. "It's bad English. It's 'I'll teach 'em'."

"We don't want to teach 'em!" growled Badger. "We want to learn 'em! Now, here's Mole back again."

"I've had such fun!" said Mole, who was most excited. "I saw Toad's washerwoman clothes hanging up to dry, so I put them on and went down to Toad Hall. When the sentries stopped me, I asked them if they wanted any washing done, and then I said, 'You've got a surprise coming to you'!"

"Mole, how could you?" gasped Rat in dismay. Badger put down his newspaper.

"I said, 'My daughter washes for Mr Badger'," went on Mole. "I told them, 'I've heard that a hundred bloodthirsty badgers will attack from the paddock tonight and six boatloads of armed rats will arrive from the river – and the Death-or-Glory Toads will storm the orchard. So get out while you have the chance!' By the time I went they were falling over each other to post sentries and arguing about who would have to be on duty and miss the party!"

"Mole, you've ruined it!" wailed Toad.

"Mole," said Badger quietly, "you have more sense in your little finger than some animals have in their whole bodies. Well done! Now, instead of being in the dining room, half those animals will be at the other end of the grounds and their weapons with them. Well done, Mole! Now there's nothing to do but wait until dark."

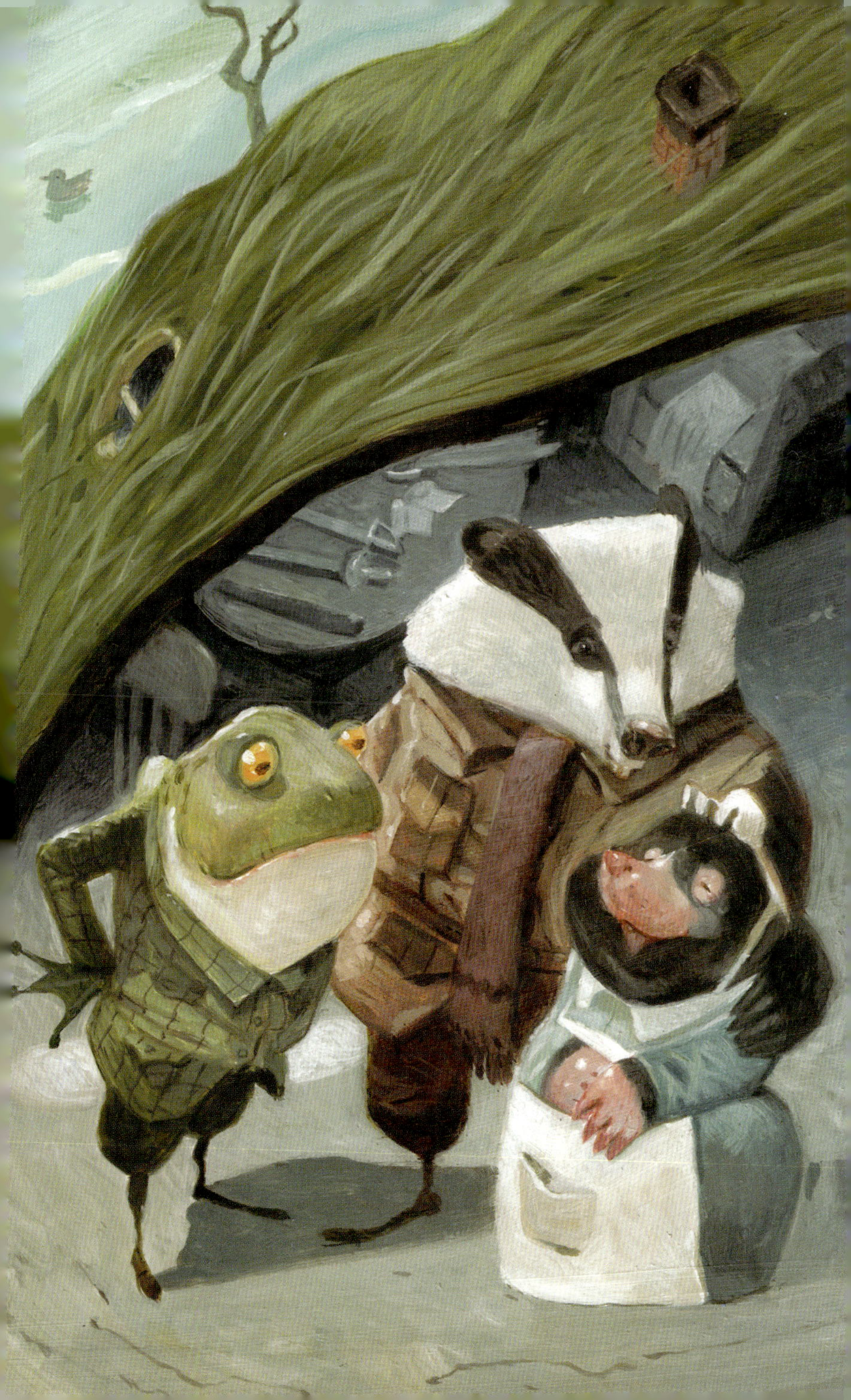

CHAPTER TEN
The Return of Mr Toad

As darkness fell, Rat offered swords and cutlasses to everyone. Badger only laughed and said that all he needed was a strong stick.

"Off we go!" he said. "Follow me! Mole first, because he's done so well today, then Rat, then you, Toad. And, Toad, keep quiet!"

Badger led them along the riverbank and ducked into a hole just above the water line. Mole and Rat followed him silently, but Toad fell into the river with a splash and a squeal, much to the annoyance of Badger, who grumbled that they should have left him behind.

After this, though, they all made their way without a sound to the trap door. As they walked further they heard voices singing and cheering, and a clattering and banging of tables; the animals above them were celebrating the Chief Weasel's birthday. The passage sloped upwards until the animals stood under the pantry floor, directly beneath the trapdoor.

"Ready, everyone?" said Badger.

Together, the four of them pushed open the trapdoor. Sticks and swords ready in their paws, they crept along the hall to the dining room door. Crouching behind it, they could hear the Chief Weasel making a speech.

"It is most kind of dear Mr Toad to let us use his house," he was saying, to the cheers and laughter of the Wild Wooders. "The honest and modest Toad!"

"The hour is come!" declared Badger, and they burst through the door.

What a squeaking and screaming of Wild Wooders! The four brave animals laid about them, whacking with their sticks so furiously that, to the terrified Wild Wooders, there

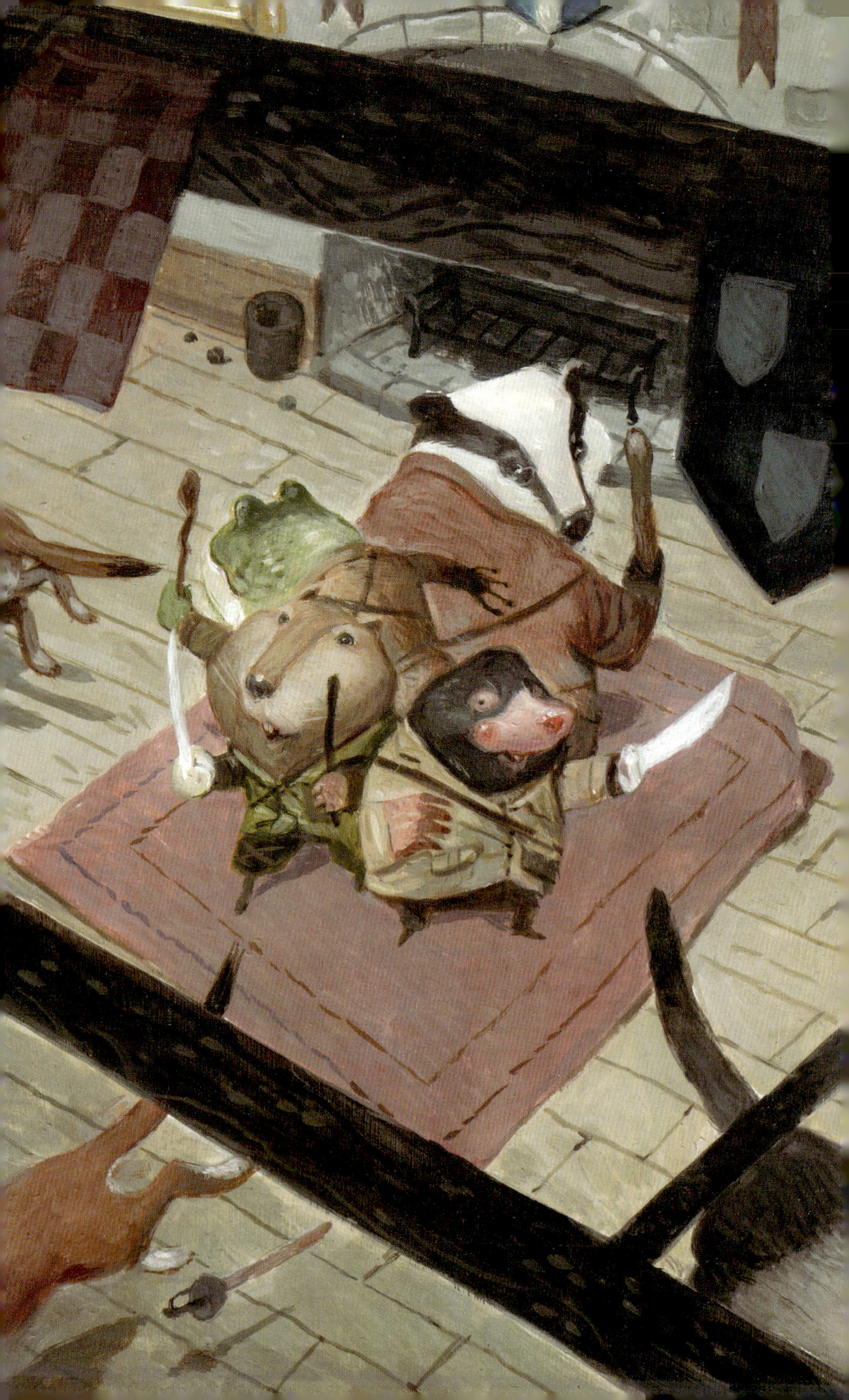

seemed to be hundreds of them.

Startled weasels, ferrets and stoats scattered. They rushed for safety, leapt out of windows and ran up the chimney, where they crammed together so tightly that several of them got stuck and had to be helped out afterwards.

It was all over very quickly. Mole rounded up the captured Wild Wooders, who, now defeated, were very glad to hand over their weapons and give themselves up, saying that it was all the fault of the Chief Weasel. Badger and Mole set them to tidying up the mess, clearing the bedrooms and making up clean beds, after which the very sorry Wild Wooders were given a bun each and set free.

"We've got your house back for you, Toad," said Badger. "Now, how about getting us some supper?"

Toad and Rat searched through the kitchen and found chicken, bread, cheese, salad and trifle. After an excellent supper they retired to comfortable beds in the grand house they had rescued by courage, tactics and the powerful use of sticks.

Toad, as usual, slept late into the morning. When he eventually came down, some cold toast and a nearly empty coffee pot remained on the table, Mole and Rat were talking and laughing in the garden and Badger was reading the newspaper. Toad felt ignored and rather put out, but, presently, Badger put the paper down.

"Toad," he said, "we must invite all our friends and neighbours to a banquet to celebrate your return. As the host, you must write out the invitations. Get them done quickly – they have to be sent out before lunch."

"What!" gasped Toad. "On a beautiful day like this? I want to go round my house, inspect it and tell everyone –" then he thought again. "Whatever you say, Badger," he said humbly. "You enjoy the sunshine. I'll do the work."

He hurried to the table and sat down. He began to write the invitations, explaining that the banquet was to welcome back the Brave and Triumphant Toad, and there would be a programme of entertainment, as follows –

T

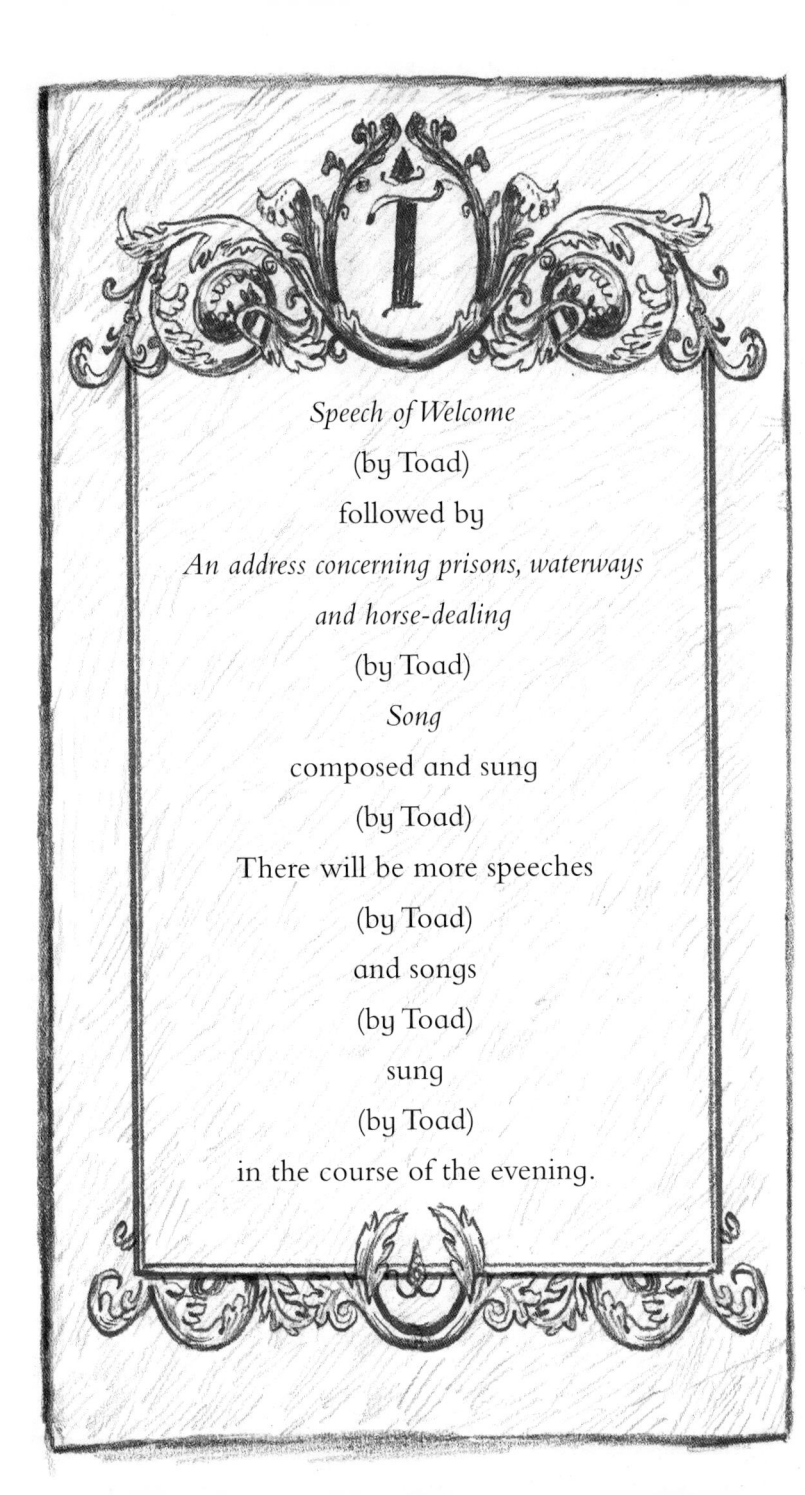

Speech of Welcome
(by Toad)
followed by
An address concerning prisons, waterways
and horse-dealing
(by Toad)
Song
composed and sung
(by Toad)
There will be more speeches
(by Toad)
and songs
(by Toad)
sung
(by Toad)
in the course of the evening.

He worked all morning, and by lunchtime the invitations were complete. A small weasel, who was very anxious to keep on the right side of Badger and his friends, was at the door asking if he could run any errands, so Toad patted him on the head and gave him the invitations to deliver.

Mole, Rat and Badger returned from the river expecting to find Toad sulking. Instead, he was so delighted that they immediately suspected him of plotting something.

He was swaggering about in the garden planning his speeches when Rat and Badger took him by the arms and marched him into the study.

"Now, Toad," said Rat, "at this banquet there will be *no* speeches and *no* songs. We're not discussing this with you. We're just telling you."

Toad saw that he was trapped. They had discovered his plan.

"Just *one* song?" he pleaded.

"Not one," said Rat firmly, though he hated himself for being harsh. "You know what your songs are like – full of boasting and exaggeration. You have to make a new start."

Toad was silent for a long time, his head down. There were tears on his face when he looked up.

"I would have liked one more evening," he said, "when I could blossom and enjoy the applause that people always give me. But you are right. I must change, and I will. But what a harsh world this is!" With his handkerchief to his face, he staggered from the room.

"I feel such a brute," said Rat.

"So do I," said Badger. "But it had to be done. He needs to be respected, and he'll be a laughing stock all his life if he doesn't learn to behave."

"It's a good thing we met that little weasel," said Rat. "I knew Toad was up to something. I read one of those invitations and confiscated the lot. Mole has written out some plain and simple ones, and we've sent those out instead."

Toad sat thoughtfully in his bedroom. At last, he smiled.

He stood up, giggling awkwardly, drew the curtains and arranged the chairs into a semi-circle.

"Ladies and gentlemen," he said to the empty chairs, "I give you – Toad's Last Song!"

Toad – came – home!
There was panic in the parlour and
  howling in the hall,
There was crying in the cow-shed and
  shrieking in the stall
When Toad – came – home!

Bang! go the drums!
The trumpeters are tooting and
  the soldiers are saluting,

*And the cannon they are shooting and
the motor cars are hooting,*
As the hero comes!

He sang it very loudly, twice. Then he smoothed down his hair and went downstairs.

He met his guests quietly and politely, and when anybody mentioned that he had been brave he only said, "Oh, I did nothing – Badger was the mastermind, and Mole and Rat did most of the fighting." When some of the animals asked for a speech he only raised a paw, shook his head, offered them more to eat and asked after their families. He was at last a completely transformed Toad.

After that, Toad, guided by his friends, sent a kind and grateful letter to the jailer's daughter with a pretty gold and pearl locket.

He thanked and compensated the engine driver and even repaid the barge-woman the cost of her horse.

After all their adventures, Badger, Rat, Mole and Toad were greatly respected by all animals, even in Wild Wood. On summer evenings they would stroll there and admiring mother weasels would bring out their children to gaze at the great Mr Toad, the gallant Rat, the famous Mr Mole and the fearsome and mighty Mr Badger.